*The Essence of*
# PSYCHOLOGY

*The Essence of*

# PSYCHOLOGY

THE MODERN BELIEFS SERIES

## Kirsten Birkett

**MATTHIAS** MEDIA
Sydney • London

Copyright © 1999 Matthias Media

St Matthias Press Ltd ACN 067 558 365

PO Box 225, Kingsford NSW Australia 2032
Telephone: (02) 9663 1478  Facsimile: (02) 9662 4289
International: +61-2-9663 1478  Facsimile: +61-2-9662 4289
E-mail: sales@matthiasmedia.com.au
Internet: http://www.matthiasmedia.com.au

St Matthias Press (UK)

PO Box 665, London SW20 8RU, England
Telephone: (0181) 942 0880  Facsimile: (0181) 942 0990
E-mail: MattMedia@compuserve.com

ISBN 1 876326 13 1

Cover design and typesetting by Joy Lankshear Design Pty Ltd.
Printed in Australia.

# Contents

# Preface

## THE MODERN BELIEFS SERIES

The world is shaped by what we believe; our values, our society, our daily activities will reflect what we believe to be true and important. This is the case for everyone, not just those who consider themselves 'religious' or 'having faith'. Whatever beliefs a person may hold, be they secular, atheist, religious, modern, traditional, scientific, artistic or a mixture of them all, that person's world view and way of life will reflect his or her ideological convictions.

Most people go through life happily (or unhappily) unaware of their beliefs. It's easy to assume that everyone else thinks the same way as me, and even easier just never to think about it at all. It's a sad way to be, both for individuals and for the society we create. If Socrates considered "the unexamined life is not worth living", we might add that "the unexamined society is not worth having"—if we don't understand what we believe and why society is the way it is, we will never be able to affect it for the better.

The 'Modern Beliefs' series aims to describe and evaluate, in an introductory way, the essence of the beliefs that pervade our world; the ideas that tell us who we are, why we are here and what we ought to do about it. There are many such ideas, most of them inherited from past ages, some newly invented.

Our world is so full of these ideas, it can be confusing just waking up in the morning. We hope that the 'Modern Beliefs' series will help to make at least a few parts of it more understandable.

## The Essence of Psychology

This short book about psychology is written to introduce the topic to those who know little about it, and particularly to Christians who are curious about the relationship between psychology and Christianity.

Because most people's contact with psychology is clinical or therapeutic, and because this is where most people have questions about it, the clinical side is dealt with first in Part I. Yet psychology was never primarily a clinical pursuit; its main aim is to predict and explain normal human behaviour through studying the mind. Part II, then, covers the emergence of experimental psychology— still a very young science—and the range of research topics it has covered. Hopefully many of the terms that float around, such as behaviourism, conditioning, psychoanalysis and so on will make more sense after reading this section. Part III then addresses the particular issues that arise from the interaction between psychology and Christianity. For although psychology is merely a study of the mind, its proponents frequently take up and champion particular theories which clash to a greater or lesser extent with Christian doctrines. For many people, psychology is an attempt to explain the mind in deliberately anti-religious terms.

The clinical and historical information in this book is neither new nor original; it would be available to anyone who cared to read through a number of psychology textbooks. What this book does is digest and summarize this material, and combine it with a Christian perspective. The Christian insights come from discussion with many biblically-informed Christians, both psychologists and those who have experience with psychological treatment, and from considered reflection upon the Bible itself.

The Bible is not a book of psychology; but what it tells us about the createdness of humanity is essential for understanding what psychology sets out to do.

*Kirsten Birkett*
June 1999

# Part 1

# PSYCHOLOGY ON THE COUCH

What is psychology? Perhaps the most famous image of psychology would be of a patient lying on a couch, speaking of their childhood while a bearded expert sits in the background nodding wisely. This is how most people probably think of psychology: pouring out your troubles to someone who just sits and nods, or at best repeats your question back to you. It's a picture often ridiculed in movies and television; the self-indulgent, neurotic patient who spends money on a 'shrink' instead of getting on with life and doing something useful.

Psychology is in fact something far more profound than this superficial picture. It is the study of the mind, and one of its applications is to treat people with illnesses of the mind. Because the issue of mental illness and counselling is probably what people immediately think of in relation to psychology, we will be looking at this area first, then going on to examine the wealth of theory and experiment that lies behind the treatment.

There are people with genuine illnesses who can be helped by the various therapies offered by applied psychology (applying theories of the mind to real-life situations). As we will see in this section, the various theories of how people and their minds function lead to various different treatments for people whose minds are not working properly.

Both clinical psychologists and psychiatrists offer treatment for mental illness. A clinical psychologist is essentially an experimental scientist, who has done a degree in researching the mind, and then done extra training in how to treat people and apply the experimentally-gained knowledge. A psychiatrist is a doctor who has done a degree in medicine, and then done extra training to find out how to treat the mind in particular. The two might offer exactly the same kinds of treatments; they may even work in the same centre. In that case, the difference can be simply that the psychiatrist (being a doctor) will be able to write drug prescriptions and the clinical psychologist will not.

In general, however, psychiatrists tend to treat the more extreme mental illnesses—the ones which might require hospitalization or heavy drug therapy. Clinical psychologists are more often found in private practice, treating those with less severe but still distressing problems for which the patient voluntarily seeks treatment. It maybe that this distinction, reinforced by certain social expectations and bureaucratic necessities, pushes people with more severe mental imbalances to a more medicalised, drug-based treatment and those with less severe problems to a talking-therapy treatment. In any case, a psychiatrist and a clinical psychologist are both interested in how disorders of the mind may be fixed, and may agree or disagree on the best method of doing it.

What does it mean to say that a person has a mental illness? This is not something that can be defined precisely, because not enough is known yet about how healthy minds function. In any case what is socially acceptable, and what is regarded as 'ill,' varies from culture to culture. Nonetheless, there are clearly ways in which people can have unhealthy minds, meaning that they have a detrimental effect on the person's life and (perhaps) other people's lives. This is not a moral judgement, but just an observed one. What exactly the problems are, how to distinguish them from other possible problems and most of all what causes them, are hazy areas. This is not surprising. Considering how complex people are, and how recently we have arrived at any sort of understanding of the nervous system and the brain, the surprising thing is that we know as much about mental health as we do. For there are, despite the complications, quite effective ways of understanding what a person's mind is doing and how that might be changed for the better.

Of course, definitions of 'better' or 'healthy' are subjective and no doubt culturally bound. In psychology, we will come across many such ideas which are difficult to pin down exactly. The important thing to remember is that just because something is not fully understood does not make it imaginary. A lot of detailed things *are* known about minds and how we use them; and there has been considerable clinical success in helping ill people live happier, more productive lives.

What do we mean by a 'mental illness'? Probably one of the most talked about recently is depression; not just 'feeling down', but an ongoing sense of hopelessness and lack of energy which the patient cannot 'get over' just by willpower. This is an example of a mood disorder. Also, people can suffer from various anxiety disorders; that is, suffering excessive anxiety and fear in situations that are not actually dangerous. For instance, people can be excessively afraid of open spaces (agoraphobia), of relating to other people (social phobia); or can just be generally and constantly anxious (general anxiety disorder). Others suffer from obsessive-compulsive disorder; the compulsion to do things over and over, such as checking the door or washing hands. People may even suffer from dissociative disorders, when they seem to dissociate different parts of themselves into separate personalities; or schizophrenia, a serious disorder in which perceptions of reality can be highly distorted.

Mental illnesses like these are not just the result of being lazy, or imagining you're sick. They occur when there is something about how your mind is working which makes your life difficult. They are as real as chicken-pox or colour-blindness. Less is known about what causes these illnesses, or how to diagnose them accurately (in some cases), but mental illnesses need not and should not have a stigma about them.

So what could be the cause of such a diverse range of problems? Is it a matter of genetics, or of how you were brought up, or whether your mother weaned you too fast, or because of some repressed emotion? The answer that a particular therapist gives, and the treatment he or she prescribes, will largely depend on which theory of the mind is held. These supposed causes and prescribed treatments can vary greatly. This, however, does not mean that psychology is all made up; it just means it's a young science, and lots of bits and pieces about mind function are known without necessarily knowing how they all fit together. Here we will describe some of the different approaches to mind illnesses, what treatments are prescribed, and how effective they have proved to be.

One thing to remember is that most counsellors, regardless of which approach they follow, will use bits of several different kinds of therapies, depending on the range of problems the patient has.

## ⟶ 1 ⟵

## FREUD AND PSYCHOANALYSIS

The most famous (and infamous) method of psychotherapy is the form of analysis developed by Sigmund Freud in the nineteenth century. It would have to be at the same time the most influential and the most controversial of all mental therapies. Because Freud has been such a major figure in study of the mind and personality, and because most non-specialists are probably rather confused about the value of his work, we will spend some time looking at his theories and how they may be assessed.

In his mature theory, Freud divided the mind into three main parts: the id—the most basic part in which are the fundamental urges for food, water, elimination, warmth, affection and sex; the ego, which deals with reality and tempers the instinctive demands of the id; and the superego, in which are moral standards inculcated by society, which put

17

pressure on the ego. The human being as conceptualized by Freud is a complex interplay of three psychic systems, which cannot always be reconciled. There is also a fixed amount of mental 'energy' which the three parts compete for. Freud thought most of the problems people face come from this competition, which is almost entirely unconscious. The only thing that emerges into consciousness is the problem which is the result of the conflict.

Childhood is also considered crucial in creating or preventing mental problems. In Freud's theory, a child goes through different stages in which the id is satisifed through different parts of the body. First is the oral; after weaning, the anal is the most important; then the phallic stage. At adulthood the genital stage is reached in which heterosexual interests predominate. At each stage there is bound to be some conflict between what the id wants and what the environment will provide; and the way in which these conflicts are resolved determines basic personality traits. So, for instance, if there is a problem during toilet-training and the child thus does not proceed from this stage, the adult will be an anal personality with certain uptight characteristics. The most serious problems come from the phallic stage, when a child is overcome with desire for the parent of the opposite sex and must cope with society's taboos on this; Freud thought that many people never got over this stage, developing an 'Oedipal complex'. Freud called this 'freezing' of development at a certain stage 'fixation'.

Freud thought that early childhood trauma—which

he thought usually occurred in fantasy, not reality—was the underlying cause for many adult neuroses. Because the unacceptable impulses were repressed in childhood they were never made available to adult scrutiny, and so remained infantile and intense.

Freud has been criticized by almost every kind of psychologist since. Essentially, most of the theory is impossible to prove or disprove; Freud made it up, and there's no actual test you can do to find out if he was right. It may be thought that the clinical experience of a therapist who treats many patients could provide evidence; but this would be highly suspect, for patients are almost inevitably strongly influenced by their counsellor. Freud, moreover, based his theories on clinical experience with his patients, who were nearly all from the upper middle class of early twentieth-century Vienna, and all seeking help. This is hardly a representative base from which to make universal claims about human nature. His theoretical structures, the id, ego and superego, have no experimental evidence for their existence.

*Freud's career*
The fact is, a great deal of Freud's success appears to have come from his talent as a publicist. A little of his personal history throws some light on this claim.

Freud was highly ambitious, and gained an early reputation for himself as an excellent researcher in physiology. As it was unlikely he would receive an academic chair, he went into private practice, which necessitated getting practical experience at the Vienna General Hospital. In 1883 he went to work in the psychiatric department. This led Freud into neuroanatomy and neurology (that is, the study of the nervous system).

In 1884 Freud came across the unresearched drug cocaine. Apparently he regarded this as an excellent opportunity to gain some level of fame, through introducing the powers of a new drug to the medical fraternity. Unfortunately, his desire for publication exceeded his care for research. He began singing the praises of the drug on the basis of almost no investigation, and rushed into print stating that cocaine was not addictive. He prescribed cocaine for a patient and close friend of his to cure him of his heroin addiction, and claimed success for the cure—despite the fact that his friend had by then reached a state of physical and financial destitution due to his dependence on cocaine.

This episode on its own has nothing to do with the value of his psychoanalytic theory. However it was apparently the beginning of a very unfortunate pattern in Freud's professional career. With supreme confidence in his theories, Freud showed a tendency to ignore (or simply not to have) experimental results, and to publish with little care for empirical research.

Freud's career was not much damaged by his publications on cocaine. He went to Paris to study with the neurologist Jean Charcot. It was because of Charcot's theories of hysteria that Freud began to develop his psychoanalytic theory. Freud returned to Vienna with Charcot's belief that ideas could lodge in an unconscious portion of the mind, where they could be transformed into bodily symptoms. More recent research has revealed that this doctrine of Charcot's had entirely false foundations—his own research methods left a lot to be desired—but it still shaped the course of twentieth-century psychiatry.

A further step along Freud's path to psychoanalytic theory was his work with Joseph Breuer, who published a case that was to become archetypal in psychoanalysis. His patient, referred to as Anna O, showed extreme symptoms such as an inability to drink, paralysis and screaming fits. Breuer claimed that under hypnosis Anna O was able to relive the causes of these symptoms—to do with traumatic episodes with her father—and on waking, was cured of the dramatic symptoms.

Anna O was not actually cured by Breuer. She remained extremely ill. Breuer evidently overlooked or ignored the evidence for neurological malfunction; and published that she had been cured when she was still confined to a sanatorium. The odd thing is that Freud was quite aware that Anna O was not cured; nonetheless he used this as his founding case of psychoanalysis.

It must be recognised that neurology was far less detailed in those days. Certain crucial diagnostic tools were not invented until the twentieth century. Brain deficiencies, tumours, and chemical imbalances could not be discovered, and so problems they caused were frequently ascribed to other causes. Freud's alternative theories, however, have survived well into the present day despite their shaky origins. Freud diagnosed many as having hysteria, a specific disease in which some hidden physical mechanism transformed the nervous energy created by emotional traumas into physical symptoms. The existence of this sort of 'mechanism' is now totally discredited among psychologists.

One of the reasons for the success of his theory was that Freud's technique had mechanisms for explaining away failure embedded in it. For instance, if the patient did not fully recount the traumatic event which supposedly caused the hysteria, then the cure would not work fully; and that was the patient's fault, not Freud's. Moreover, the case histories show that Freud would insist there was a history of (say) masturbation in a patient, even if the patient denied it, and would put this down as fact regardless of the patient's testimony. In fact, childhood seduction was taken to be the cause of trauma only if the patient *could not* remember it. His theories were self-confirming; the patient's inability to remember a case of seduction was proof of its reality. His case histories also demonstrate that his therapeutic method consistently failed to work; his patients didn't get better.

Some of Freud's ideas have been fruitful. The idea of the unconscious, for instance, is certainly appealing. However, it is not really new to Freud—as long as we have had human literature, the idea has been expressed that people's motives are often obscure, even to themselves.

However other facets of Freud's theories which were

thought for a long time to be common-sense have recently been challenged. The idea that expressing repressed emotions, reliving traumatic experiences and so on is therapeutic has been challenged of more recent times. It is simply not the case that reliving a traumatic event will necessarily help one 'get over' or 'work through' the trauma. It may just re-emphasize the damaging emotions.

### Psychoanalysis today

It may be that Freud's ideas were ill-founded; but what of psychoanalysis today? It is still certainly very popular. Since Freud, psychoanalytic thinking has changed in important ways, but all treatments have some basic tenets in common. Classical psychoanalysis is based on the idea that neurotic anxiety is the reaction of the ego when a previously repressed id impulse wants to be expressed. Psychoanalysis attempts to remove the earlier repression and to help the patient face the childhood conflict, and resolve it in the light of adult reality. The problem is essentially located in the past event, which needs to be uncovered and remembered before the problem can be solved. A successful treatment in psychoanalysis creates conditions whereby these troublesome inclinations can be experienced consciously, and integrated into the ego where they can be controlled and modified.

These conditions to lift the repression involve various techniques. One is free association—randomly saying whatever comes into your mind without thinking about it first. The idea is that, because you are loosening some of the conscious control over where your thoughts take you, the unconscious thoughts may be more free to emerge. Another technique is dream analysis; assuming that your unconscious problems may be expressed in dreams, in symbols. The therapist tries to interpret these symbols to find out what is 'really' on your mind. Getting at these unconscious impulses can take a long time. Treatment can extend over several years, with as many as five sessions a week.

One of the key roles of the therapist is interpretation. At the right time, which the analyst will identify through experience and instinct, the analyst begins to point out things like the underlying meaning of dreams. If it is offered too early the patient might reject it, and leave treatment. To be effective, interpretations should reflect insights that the patient is on the verge of making himself. Interpretations are held to be particularly helpful in establishing the meaning of resistances that disturb the patient's free association. If a patient denies an interpretation, that is often taken as a sign that the therapist's interpretation is correct. This is one of the biggest problems in psychoanalysis. How is it that the therapist knows that 'no' is really 'yes'? How can the therapist actually know better than the patient what the patient is thinking? There is a great capacity for abuse here, no matter how experienced and empathetic the therapist is.

A crucial part of psychoanalytic therapy is the 'transference neurosis'. This is when the patient reaches the stage where he or she will sometimes act towards the therapist in an emotion-charged and irrational way. This is taken to mean that the patient is transferring to the therapist emotions that he or she has from people in the past who were probably important in creating the problem. In psychoanalysis, transference is regarded as essential to a complete cure. When analysts notice transference developing they take hope that the important neurotic conflict from childhood is being approached. Analysts encourage transference by deliberately remaining shadowy figures. They sit behind the patient, and reveal as little as possible of their own personal lives.

Counter-transference is the feeling of the analyst toward the patient. Analysts have to make sure that they understand their own motivations well enough to be able to 'see' the client clearly. For this reason, part of the formal training of analysts is to be thoroughly psychoanalysed themselves. They must not have any repressed problems which might cause them to react in a wrong way towards their patients. Moreover, analysts must not become actively involved in helping patients with everyday problems. Short-term relief, such as a suggestion on how to cope with a particular problem, might deflect the patient's efforts to uncover the repressed conflicts. So for an analyst to say anything helpful is considered to be counter-productive. (This is directly opposite to cognitive behaviour therapy, which we will discuss below.)

It is probably clear by now why so many psychologists have deep reservations about psychoanalysis. It relies on a theory with no evidence for it, and it involves treatments which seem quite counter-intuitive. The crucial question is, then, does it work? After all these years, does it actually help people get better from their problems?

The difficulty is that, just as the theory is impossible to test, so is the therapy. How can it be demonstrated that a repression has been lifted—that the childhood problem that was actually the cause has been reached? How can it be tested whether the unconscious works as psychotherapy says? The insights, or uncovered conflicts, that the patient reaches seem to be very much influenced by what the therapist is looking for. Freudians tend to find that most of their patients reach oedipal insights. Some argue that maybe it doesn't matter whether the insight is true, as long as it helps the patient change and feel better. After all, it is impossible to know with any degree of certainty whether an event really happened, and if it did whether it caused the current problem. For some so-called childhood memories, this might be irrelevant; but when the uncovered memory is something like childhood sexual abuse, it becomes extremely important whether it actually happened. There is absolutely no guarantee that the memories regained will be true, and not suggested by the therapist.

Despite the difficulties in determining whether psychoanalysis 'works', some studies have been done which try to determine what rate of patients are actually helped by their therapy. One thing that appears to be evident is that severe problems such as schizophrenia do not respond as well as anxiety disorders. Also, the more education a patient has the better he or she will do, probably because so much of the therapy relies on verbal interaction. Yet the evidence is conflicting whether the outcome of psychoanalysis is any better than what would be achieved through the mere passage of time, or by other professional help (such as a GP). This is not to say that it does no good, but clear evidence is lacking. It is a very complex question after all, given the great diversity in patients and therapists, and the extremely long time that therapy can take.

## ═2═

## PHYSIOLOGICAL THERAPY

Although Freud has been immensely influential on the practice of clinical psychology, there are many other approaches which have had considerable success in competing with the psychoanalytic approach. One which has gained prominence with recent research techniques is the basic physiological understanding. Some mental illnesses have come to be regarded as primarily a physical problem; that there is some physiological problem in the brain which needs to be treated through chemical (drugs) or physical (surgery) intervention. There has been a large amount of research in this area, leading to some important findings. For instance, schizophrenia is probably affected by heredity. Depression may result from a failure of certain neural transmitters. Anxiety disorders may stem from a defect within the autonomic nervous system. Certain brain syndromes may be caused by damaged structures of the brain. The important consequence of such conclusions is that these disorders may be treated through surgery or drugs which fix the damaged systems. Sometimes definite improvements have been shown through these sorts of treatments, even if it is not known exactly why they work; and sometimes non-physiological treatments can help even when the cause is physiological (for example, relaxation therapy for anxiety disorders).

A great many practitioners regard mental illness as consisting of a background predisposition, plus a trigger that sets off the illness. This seems to fit most illnesses, which cannot be reduced to one single cause. So, a person may have an inherited predisposition to be an anxious, nervy kind of person; then a particularly stressful series of events causes them to develop a particular phobia. Or it could be that a person has a naturally gloomy frame of mind, maybe because of some chemical imbalance or because of having a sad childhood, but will not necessarily become depressed until something goes wrong—they lose a job, or experience some physical illness.

## 3

## BEHAVIOURAL THERAPY

Behaviourism is both an experimental approach to the study of the mind as well as a theory of how people function (and therefore how problems might be treated). It is the theory that relies on 'stimulus and response'—studying what response organisms have to a given environmental stimulus. These days behaviourism has quite a bad name, because of the excesses of some of the behaviourists—insisting that humans are 'nothing but' stimulus and response, as for instance B. F. Skinner is famous for saying.

However this bad reputation can hide the fact that behavioural psychology has uncovered a lot of material about why people behave the way they do, and especially how they learn to act in certain ways rather than others. It was originally hoped, early this century, that through behavioural studies human behaviour could eventually be predicted and controlled. Fortunately this stage has not been reached, and is not likely to be (although finding out how much your behaviour is manipulated in, for instance, shopping centres and grocery stores, can be quite alarming!).

In behavioural theory, a lot of work has been done on how learning comes about through conditioning (remember Pavlov's famous salivating dogs). Similar work has been done on how to extinguish behaviour—that is, how to get an animal (or person) to unlearn some behaviour that has been learned. There are other techniques as well as conditioning, but the basic idea is that we learn behaviours through certain experimentally verified methods.

This is important in therapy, for it is assumed that abnormal or problematic behaviour is learned in the same manner as most other human behaviour. This is not something that can necessarily be proven; for instance, a psychologist might surmise that depression was learned through years of reinforcement, but without observing everything the person did and experienced all those years, it is impossible to know for sure. Nonetheless, the essential assumption of behavioural therapy is that if something can be learned, then it can be unlearned. What is more, this therapy has been shown many times to work. Regardless of what actually did cause the problem—depression, phobia, chronic anxiety—people can learn not to act in the ways that continue the problem.

Behavioural therapies, then, include such things as counter-conditioning; so for a phobia, the patient may be exposed to the feared situation but in small doses, or in a way that the reaction is more likely to be positive than negative. Another part of this is systematic desensitization—gradually giving the patient larger and larger doses of the feared situation, so that the patient gets used to it and loses the fear. For problems such as social phobia, where the person is afraid to interact with other people, the patients may be given assertion training which encourages them to speak up and react appropriately. Another technique is modelling, in which the patients watch others do the feared thing—for instance, handling snakes. Role-playing can perfom a similar function. There are applications for group situations: for instance, most teachers would realise that rewarding socially acceptable behaviour, while ignoring unacceptable behaviour, encourages the children to act well.

## ═4═

# COGNITIVE THERAPY

Cognitive psychology is the new and growing trend in the study of the mind. It emerged partly as a reaction to behaviourism, which focussed almost exclusively on the behaviour (response) that resulted when a stimulus was applied. Cognitive psychology, in contrast to this emphasis, wants to know instead what is happening *in the mind* between stimulus and response. It focuses on how people structure their experiences and make sense of them. For instance, our minds don't just store an unrelated set of facts. We fit new information into an already present framework or schema; and, in turn, the schema may be altered to fit new information. Cognitive psychologists study how we acquire, store and use information.

Cognitive psychology has only recently been applied to therapy, but with very postive results. For instance, a widely held view of depression now places the blame on a cognitive 'set' or framework of thinking: the individual's overriding sense of hopelessness.

There are some theoretical problems with the cognitive approach to therapy. Some concepts such as 'schema' or 'cognitive set' are not always well defined. Also, they do not necessarily explain much—saying depression arises from a negative schema is really just saying that depressed people think gloomy thoughts, which is in fact part of the diagnosis of depression. However, what is distinctive in cognitive psychology is that the *thoughts* are given causal

31

status for some of the other problems, such as sadness. So changing the thoughts, it is assumed, can lift the feeling of sadness. Where the negative schema came from in the first place remains unanswered. It is enough to identify that at the moment the sad emotional state is being maintained by thinking gloomy thoughts. Why the person started this gloomy mindset is not regarded as crucial. In this way cognitive theory is quite different from psychoanalysis, which assumes that only by *knowing* where the problem came from can it be cured. Cognitive theory, on the other hand, takes the problem as it is and looks for ways to fix it.

Cognitive therapy has recently gained widespread attention. Often used in conjunction with behaviour therapy, it tries to change the *thinking* processes of the patients, in order to influence their emotions and behaviour. For instance, irrational beliefs can lead to people placing excessive demands on themselves. If a person believes that he or she must perform perfectly in order to have the approval of others, then that person will most likely have a miserably high-pressured life, which can lead to depression. If that person can change the *belief*—the actual thought—then the problem can be relieved.

Although the cognitive and behavioural models are different, therapists usually combine the two. Both approaches to therapy are closely linked with experimental research. Both demand rigorous standards of proof. This gives people some confidence in cognitive-behavioural therapy, for it is well researched and only uses techniques that have been shown to 'work'.

Cognitive-behavioural therapy consists of a number of different elements that work together to help overcome mental problems. One such element is counter-conditioning. If you have learned (been 'conditioned') to react negatively in a certain situation, counter-conditioning therapy puts you in that situation but with some means of making a more positive response—for instance, having learned deep relaxation techniques. Every time you face the feared situation, you are prepared with a deep relaxation technique, so you are far less likely to experience the negative, panicky response you had previously learned. In time, the situation will simply fail to elicit that response. This does not have to involve facing the real-life situation, although that is most effective. Usually facing the fear might be done through imagination in a therapy session, with homework of facing increasingly frightening real-life situations.

The cognitive element of the therapy involves cognitive restructuring: that is, changing a pattern of thought that is presumed to be causing a negative emotion or behaviour. We all have instinctive underlying beliefs about ourselves, usually things we take for granted and don't examine. It could be, however, that these beliefs are quite irrational and negative, and lead to fearful or depressive emotions. For instance, depressed people might have the underlying, ongoing thought, 'I'm worthless, I can't do anything'. A highly-strung, workaholic person might have the belief 'Everyone must accept me or else I'm a failure'. Regardless of how the person came to have these beliefs, the therapist teaches the patient to substitute rational self-statements. The goal is to make it part of everyday thinking. It is not assumed that someone can change their thoughts or beliefs instantaneously, especially as these patterns of thought might have been held over a lifetime. However by consciously identifying these beliefs, and challenging them consistently and frequently, especially when a difficult situation is coming up, patterns of thinking can be changed. So much of our thinking is a matter of habit; it can be changed with practice.

Research shows that even this on its own is beneficial, and when combined with the various behavioural therapies is highly effective. What controversy there is, is ethical rather than practical. That is, some people are uncomfortable about the right of the therapist to decide what is 'rational' thinking; or even that 'rational' is always good. After all, the therapist is dictating to the patient what he or she should hold as fundamental beliefs. This is no less a problem in any other kind of therapy, where the assumptions of the therapist are usually highly influential in determining the outcome; but it is more obvious in cognitive therapy. On the other hand, perhaps by making the desired beliefs conscious and stated up-front, the patient has more freedom to decide which direction he or she will move in.

A slightly different kind of cognitive therapy attempts to change negative patterns of thinking through challenging its errors in logic. The basic idea is to discover the 'automatic' thoughts that run through our minds constantly. Everyone will have automatic thoughts for any event; most people will have positive, or neutral thoughts ('Well look at that, a bus full of people') but people suffering depression or other ailments will probably have negative thoughts ('Look at that bus full of people, everyone has more friends than I do'). Challenging these thoughts involves deliberately identifying them and replacing the negative with a neutral or positive thought.

## ⊰5⊱

## HUMANISTIC THERAPY

We now come to the fourth major trend in psychological treatment today. This is the self-help therapy that has become very popular through innumerable books and groups. It assumes that people are basically healthy and good, with an innate drive for growth and self-actualization. When a person is not happy and functional, that must be because he or she has somehow denied this basic drive. Humanistic psychology emphasizes that the person has to reach self-fulfilment regardless of social judgements. Carl Rogers was one of the leading figures in establishing this movement. 'Rogerian' therapy has come to be known for its positive, accepting style. Rogers thought that we have an innate tendency to realise potentials. Because of this very positive view of people, he assumed that people's own decisions would not only make them happy, but would also turn them into good, civilized people.

Humanist therapy tries to help people to get in touch with their inner selves, their true feelings, and learn to express them without undue concern for what others think. The patients are expected to be responsible for much of their own treatment—therapists do not impose goals, but help clients to discover their own basic natures and make their own judgements about what they need to do to enhance themselves. Such decisions are assumed to be good ones. The basic tool of the therapist is unconditional positive regard, complete acceptance and respect for the client's feelings and actions. Because patients must take responsibility for themselves, the therapist must refrain from giving advice. If the therapist steps in, the process of growth and self-actualization will only be thwarted. Most of all therapists try to be empathetic.

However, while therapists are not to impose goals, their empathy is more than just being sympathetic; it can take a directional role when the therapist suggests why the client is not fulfilling their potential with their current behaviour. The idea is that the client will eventually adopt a new framework because the old one was faulty.

There have been numerous studies attempting to evaluate client-centred therapy. Rogers had a great emphasis on research and empirical evaluation. However research has yielded inconsistent results, mainly casting doubt on Rogers's own assumption that success is mainly dependent on the therapist's empathy, genuineness and warmth. It seems that patients need more than an accepting, loving therapist in order to get better.

Many people have also recognised the flaws in the basic assumptions of humanist therapy. For instance, if self-actualisation is humanity's primary motivation, then why do so many people put themselves in situations where they learn faulty frameworks? The biggest problem is, however, that people are demonstrably not intrinsically good. Left to their own determination, people will usually want to do selfish things, which will not necessarily make them happy nor make them good citizens. This kind of therapy seems to offer a very positive solution to the client, but as cognitive psychology has shown, people's underlying beliefs and thoughts are often detrimental to the person and need to be changed, not affirmed.

## ═6═

## CONCLUSION

Of all the types of therapy on offer, cognitive-behavioural therapy has the best track-record as well as the most solidly established experimental basis. These techniques do work. What is more, they help in any situation when a person is likely to feel anxiety or fear, or depression, even if that person would not be diagnosed as mentally ill. Everyone goes through stressful times which can crush one's optimism. The techniques of cognitive-behavioural therapy—gradually working back up through exposure to the feared situation, identifying irrational or negative thoughts and consciously challenging them—are useful for anyone to learn.

This brings us back to the question of what psychology *is*. For although most people think of psychology as therapy, it is actually about the study of healthy minds. Psychology began as the effort to understand how the human mind works; the applications which help unhealthy minds get better are really secondary. Psychology is the human aim of working out how our minds operate under all conditions, not just when they are ill. This is the background world of the experimental laboratory which can often seem more mysterious than what goes on in the counselling room. It is to this largely unknown but fascinating world that we now turn.

# ⊶ *Part 2* ⊷

# PSYCHOLOGY IN
# THE LAB

Psychology is essentially the study of the human mind. What that study actually consists of has changed over time, as has the method of study. At one time the contents of the mind, or thoughts, were studied, and the main method was *introspection*—that is, people just thinking about what they were thinking, and trying to do this in a systematic and consistent way. Later, psychology developed more specifically into study of the *structures* of the mind; memory, perception and so on. We have already seen some of the study of human *behaviour,* seeking to understand what makes humans behave the way they do, regardless of what they might be thinking; such studies very precisely controlled and measured *stimuli* and *responses*. Finally and most recently, psychology has returned to studying the *inner mind,* but in a much more objective way than was possible just through introspection.

To get an overview of the study of psychology we could simply list the projects of different labs all over the world. That would be comprehensive, but perhaps incomprehensible. To better understand what is done in experimental psychology, it is very helpful to see how it developed; in that way, the words and phrases that you may have vaguely connected with psychology can be put in context. Many of the studies carried out today are highly technical and specific; but as we see how the different trends in psychology came into being and interacted, we can understand the broad picture of what is happening now.

## ✦ 1 ✦

## BEGINNINGS

Experimental psychology did not really begin until the late 1800s, but there were some important precedents which provided some of the basic research behind psychology. First of all, the physiological basis for psychology required some understanding of the nervous system. The idea that thoughts and emotions, and ordinary sensory feelings, are somehow connected through a physical system is not at all obvious. The nervous system was very mysterious for much of medical history (the fact that nerve fibres are so difficult to see in dissection was a large problem in itself).

Charles Bell and Francois Magendie did important work on nerves in 1803 and 1822 respectively. By that time there had been interest in what part of the brain controlled what, where different nerves went and so on, but without the experimental and dissecting skills and technology available today, such research was strictly limited. However, another field was developing which was to find a surprising connection with neurology—the study of electricity. By 1800, Alessandro Volta had worked out how to make batteries; and the Italian Luigi Galvani had also surprisingly discovered that electricity touching a nerve makes a muscle twitch. At this stage very little was understood about the connection, but, in a serendipitous turn of history, the physiologist Johannes Müller (1801-1858) took up the electrical idea, arguing that the nervous

42

system is based on the sending and receiving of electrical impulses. Müller's work became the standard text on physiology for generations. And more importantly, Müller had a number of brilliant students.

Emil du Bois-Reymond (1818-1896) went to work to verify Müller's conjecture and succeeded. He was a militant mechanist—a scientist who was determined to explain human beings by purely mechanical means. He was opposed to the romantic nature philosophy, which upheld ideas such as spirit, or 'vital force'. Indeed, there is a story that he, with Hermann von Helmholtz , Carl Ludwig and Ernst Brücke pledged one day in 1845 to remove all vitalistic, spiritual, and poetic explanations in physiology and have only explanations in physical or chemical terms. The significance in this story lies in identifying these men. Helmholtz was an influential physiologist, as was Ludwig; Ludwig also had as a student the famous psychologist Ivan Pavlov. Brüke became professor of physiology at the University of Vienna, where he had as a student the young Sigmund Freud.

Johannes Müller had also put forward a doctrine of specific nerve energies. He suggested that the information conveyed by a nerve depends on where the nerve comes from, but the effect the information has depends on where it goes to. Take a minute to tangle this out, for this is crucial for understanding how the brain works. We see things, not because little bits of 'vision' travel from our eyes to our brains, but because a nerve goes from the eye to the optical centre; there is nothing essentially visual about the information itself. Helmholtz extended this idea, to work on perception of colour.

## ⊷ 2 ⊷

## FROM GERMANY AND DARWIN

Meanwhile, another researcher, Ernst Weber discovered a curious but (he thought) unimportant fact: that people can detect a difference in weight of 1 part in 30 no matter how large the actual weight. Gustav Fechner (1801-1887) took this idea further. He had made himself almost blind through staring at the sun to experiment with his visual perception. While recovering from this, he was struck with the idea of how to conduct *psychological* experiments, not just physiological ones. He was the first one to realise that an observation such as Weber's law combined psychological and physical terms: on one side a physically determined amount, on the other a psychological judgement, reported by the subject. Fechner called his new realisation 'psychophysics'. He carried out many experiments, developing a good experimental method and realising the need for statistical generalisations. He worked out a mathematical way of presenting Weber's law and used it to develop a scale of perceptual intensity mathematically, not just experimentally.

The German Wilhelm Wundt took over this fledgling discipline and turned it into a university department. He was a doctor who returned to research and worked on muscle movement with Müller. After that, he became

Helmholtz's lab assistant at Heidelberg. Eventually he moved to Leipzig as a philosopher. He set up a lab in 1879 and called it the 'Institute of Experimental Psychology'. This is usually taken as the beginning of the discipline of psychology. Max Friedrich was the first PhD in psychology in 1881. He founded the journal *Philosophical Studies*, later renamed *Psychological Studies*. Wundt also wrote on the psychology of language, and myths, religion and culture and so on—what we might call social or cultural psychology (this was synthetic work, not his own research). He also wrote straight philosophical works, *Logic*, *Ethics* and *System of Philosophy*, as well as numerous papers. He had over a hundred PhD students, including Americans who set up the discipline in America. At this stage, we have gathered all the essential elements for the establishment of psychology as a scientific discipline. There were lecturers, PhDs, laboratories and a journal. Wundt published and theorized for sixty years, and it is only seventy years since his death to now—this puts the history of psychology into perspective! This one key founding member of the discipline was theorizing for nearly half the whole history of experimental psychology.

It is interesting that the explosion in psychology all took place in Germany; it did not take hold in any other part of northern Europe, nor in England. Cambridge and Oxford were extremely conservative. In Germany and the United States, it was partly the flexibility of the university system that enabled psychology to take hold.

However, from England was to come a concept which

has dominated psychology ever since; that is, Darwinism. Darwin was a contemporary of Fechner and Wundt. While some of his work contributed directly to psychology (his *The Expression of the Emotions in Man and Animals*, 1872, provided a lot of information about emotion; also he published a diary of observations of his first child's development), Darwin's main impact was conceptual. The notion of the continuity of species implied that intelligence and instinct were on a continuum, not two entirely different phenomena. Darwin's naturalism also put humans firmly in the realm of 'science'—understood, of course, as entirely materialistic science.

Also from England came the work of Francis Galton (1822-1911), who was actually Darwin's cousin. He had numerous intellectual interests (for instance, he was the first to persuade Scotland Yard to use fingerprints for identification). He was interested in the idea of inherited variation, in particular for psychological traits. As the evidence for his theory that psychological qualities were inherited, he collected data on distinguished men. When he found that they tended to be clumped in family lines, this appeared to support his conclusion. (His research had some flaws: Galton ignored sociological factors such as how much money and what good connections these men would have started off with; and it evidently never occurred to him to ask why these families had no eminent women.) Galton had no research programme or theories, but collected immense amounts of data and so gave a boost to psychological thinking.

## ⊷3⊷

# IN THE UNITED STATES

In the United States, psychology probably started with the philosopher William James. He had an interesting group of friends at Harvard, who called themselves the Metaphysical Society. Amongst many other things, they discussed psychological issues.

In 1875, James started teaching psychology in the physiology department, and was eventually made professor of psychology in the philosophy department. He did no research, but wrote insightfully and inspired his students to do psychology. One of Wundt's earliest students, Hugo Münsterberg, arrived at the philosophy department in 1892 and eventually took over the psychology work from James. He was very influential in the popular perception of psychology in America, a leader in psychotherapy, eyewitness testimony, patriotism, ethnic, gender and national differences and the psychology of movies. He rarely had data for his pronouncements, but nonetheless he was effectively the founder of applied psychology.

The German approach of Wundt was to have a great effect in America, seeing as his laboratory was for many years virtually the only source of PhDs in psychology. American graduate students would almost inevitably travel to Germany to gain their qualifications. Nonetheless, the Americans were always determined to be independent in their research. They rebelled against restrictions on what they were to study, and had much more of a 'free-market' response to psychological research, an approach which came to be known as 'functionalism'.

The trouble was that functionalism was not a theory as such; it was more or less saying that the brain does what it does according to what seems best. Also it provided no research programme; students were free to research whatever they felt like—so they did. A whole range of research began all over the country. Some looked at details of behaviour, some looked at large scale behaviour. There was a distinct freedom from predispositions and methodological commitments.

## ⊱ 4 ⊰

## FREUD ARRIVES

Meanwhile, another young scientist in Vienna was developing ideas which were to dominate the image of psychology for years. Sigmund Freud became interested in the workings of the mind, and worked with male hysteria in Paris; but he was moving into a new kind of psychology. He started a private practice specializing in nervous diseases, and for financial reasons decided to treat neuroses rather than organic problems. He started working with hypnosis.

As a theory, Freud's psychoanalysis was very rich and powerful, because it could explain almost anything. Although Freud portrayed himself as the lone fighter for truth, his theory was in fact tremendously popular from the start. In 1909 he spoke in America and it began to spread there. By 1940, Freud's writings provided the basic concepts for clinical psychology and personality theory. What seemed to grab people's interest was that it 'did away with' rationality; it produced a discrepancy between what people thought were their motivations and what they really were. Freud extended this from individuals to everything in society, morality and religion.

Most psychoanalysts now have to be doctors first and then specialise. This was contrary to what Freud thought; he wanted psychologists to own psychoanalysis so it would not be entombed.

## ⊷5⊷

## WATSON, SKINNER AND THE END OF THOUGHT

Despite the impact of psychoanalysis, experimental psychology still had strong roots in America. The enormous breadth of research done under functionalism eventually gave way to behaviourism, a doctrine that insisted that psychology should study behaviour alone. While the ridiculous extremes of this doctrine were probably not true of most behaviourist researchers, behaviourism did tend to ignore mental processes in favour of the actual behaviour an animal exhibited. This was a welcome message in what had become a fairly messy discipline. It set good, definable limits, and enabled accuracy and precise method.

The beginnings of behaviourism came from observations of how animals learn. In 1898, Edward Lee Thorndike had studied learning in cats, with an experiment that involved a cat learning how to get out of a box with a door. He suggested that learning was a smooth curve; a mechanical 'stamping in' of association. It was not an understanding of *ideas*, because then we would see a sudden jump in performance when the cat suddenly tumbled to the idea of how to open the box. Rather it was a mechanical connection between the stimulus and the response which was gradually reinforced. This was the essence of behaviourism. Other people had talked about stimulus and response, but had allowed for associations linking different stimuli and linking ideas to stimuli and to response. Thorndike, however, said that what was happening was *only* stimulus-response. The cat was not 'thinking' about opening the box; it was automatically learning as the stimulus was repeatedly applied. This was a major turning point. It took the control of behaviour out of the head and put it in the environment. Stimuli and responses are out there where they can be manipulated and recorded.

Thorndike then turned to human learning. He had several themes: that learning always involved the acquisition of new stimulus-response associations; that these were acquired by the automatic effect of reinforcement; and that the thoughts and intentions of the person played virtually no role in learning. As long as a response was reinforced it did not matter whether the subject knew what was happening.

John Watson (1878-1958) claimed in a famous publication that, essentially, behaviour is all there is. There is no 'mind' in psychology; 'mind' is not a scientific entity. Watson was professor at Johns Hopkins University by the age of 31 and editor of *Psychological Review*. Under his considerable influence, psychology threw out emotions, motives, instinct, pleasure and pain; all of these were nothing more than stimuli that arise from within the body. Watson became the leader of American psychology.

Watson also did away with 'thinking'. We do not think, the theory might say; we just think we are thinking. There are a lot of tiny stimuli which determine our responses, which we erroneously label as thinking; but they are not mental, they are just tiny muscle activities and so on. All emotional problems are just a matter of stimulus-response learning, and so psychoanalysis is wrong. Although the many problems with this approach seem obvious now, at the time the theory was met with wild enthusiasm. It was coherent, it was neat, it provided an understandable and fundable research programme.

B. F. Skinner (1904-90) developed behaviourism to its height. He was a radical behaviourist in that he did not even want intermediate physical mechanisms such as muscle twitches included in the theory. There was simply stimulus followed by response; nothing more. The message of this doctrine was: control the reinforcer and you control the behaviour. It was a radical environmentalism which asserted that everything we are is determined by our environment and the stimulus it supplies. Skinner was a determined and ambitious thinker, who seems to have honestly thought that the whole world would be better if only it would listen to what he was saying. Skinner's disciples in universities taught only Skinnerian behaviourism, and moved into psychological clinics and educational psychology, a development which Skinner himself heartily approved of.

## ⚜ 6 ⚜

## COGNITIVE DISSENT

By 1950, behaviourism of one form or another controlled most psychological research. There was, however, dissent from a few cognitive psychologists—which at this stage meant essentially anyone who disagreed with behaviourism. Biologists in particular began to challenge the behaviourist theories of animal learning. Indeed, it was pointed out that some of the behaviouristic conclusions had actually ignored normal animal behaviour—the psychologists, eager to prove their theory and unfamiliar with what the animals normally did anyway, jumped to conclusions. Linguist Noam Chomsky showed that the behaviourist explanation of how children learn language was woefully inadequate. At the same time, computing and engineering ideas, such as information and feedback, were becoming more part of the research vocabulary. The analogies of computer programming were very influential.

Essentially what cognitive psychology did was to open the floodgates again. No longer were people restricted to controlled stimulus-response; they could theorise about what thought processes or other mental events were happening as people learned, remembered, perceived or whatever. There is still no overriding cognitive theory; no generally accepted model of what the mind is like. Nonetheless, cognitive psychology is characterized by its insistence that the mind is real and does something—which behaviourism had, especially in its extreme forms, denied.

## ⟿ 7 ⟿

## FROM THE LAB TO THE COUCH

Psychology as *treatment* was slow to begin. The first to call himself a clinical psychologist was Lightner Witmer (1867-1956) at Pennsylvania University. His 'psychological clinic' was established in 1896. By 1914 there were a few clinics at other universities. These clinics gradually came to be involved in measuring and testing intelligence, and in the mental health movement.

Up until then, the only people who had treated the mentally ill were psychiatrists. Through the late 1800s they had taken a strong mechanistic stand on mental illness; it was disease of the nervous system. Treatment was usually diet or rest. A lot of psychiatrists merely supervised the custodial care of chronic patients. As experimental psychology began to expand, however, some psychiatrists brought in psychologists as consultants or assistants. The psychiatrists were still very much in charge—the psychologists were helping out, they were not 'doing' the therapy.

Slowly psychiatrists began to take on more invasive treatments, apart from diet and rest. They used drugs and shock treatment, and surgery such as frontal lobotomies. As Freud's psychological ideas began to circulate, some illnesses were seen as not so much physiological after all. Other ideas of what might be factors in mental illness also began to gain currency; things such as family problems, economic security and so on, were seen as causal agents. Many psychiatrists began looking at mental illness in more psychological ways.

One real breakthrough for clinical psychologists came with World War II. This breakthrough was largely political. During the war some of the top psychologists were used to test and train troops for different jobs. Some of these psychologists were politically astute, and made sure the government appreciated how important psychology had been for winning the war. As soldiers started coming home there was a big need for counselling, and the psychiatric community could not cope—and with the successful lobbying, the psychological community was handed the problem, and the funds to go with it. The government gave a lot of money to universities to produce, quickly, a batch of new therapists. A new standard was needed; it was decided at a conference in Boulder, Colorado, in 1949, that these new therapists would be graduate students who had trained as psychologists first and clinicians second. They had to do a research PhD as well as a clinical internship. (There is still wrangling over this method of certification in different countries, but something like it, holds in most places today.)

Around the same time, psychology was also gaining prominence through the development of intelligence and personality tests. This was not therapy as such, but the testing and measurement of normal populations for employment or other purposes. This lead to what we now call industrial or organisational psychology.

This growing profile of psychology created real tension. The MD psychiatrists were still in charge of mental therapy, although they had no research qualifications. The PhD psychologists knew their research, but were considered lower in rank when it came to the patients (and a lot of them were not necessarily good at research anyway, since all along they had wanted to be clinicians). Gradually the psychologists were accepted as therapists. They were still not allowed to do Freudian therapy, but could do anything else. They could also go into private practice.

At around this time (that is, the 1950s), Freud's was the dominant theory in use in *clinical* psychology. However, the doors were opening. When Carl Rogers brought along his new patient-centred therapy, even though it had little theory, it still intrigued some. The behaviourists had a lot of theory and experimental backing and were very popular, and their applications had a strong influence. As more and more psychologists entered clinical practice, the therapies became more diverse and the variety of approaches now in use developed.

The therapeutic applications of psychology have affected most of society, and have shaped our vocabulary, our self-perceptions and our ways of describing ourselves. Psychology now had many faces—such as sports psychology, organizational psychology, industrial psychology, relationship counselling, and forensic psychology.

However psychological research still goes on and is still breaking new ground constantly. The applications may be the public face of psychology, but if they are to have any credence they must rest on the research that seeks to understand the human brain.

How reliable is this research? As with any science, the reliability of the findings depends on the design of the experiment, the care with which it is carried out and the validity of the analysis and interpretation of results. In other words: psychologists, like other scientists, do their best to find out the truth about their subject area. Because the mind is such a personally important, and still very mysterious, entity, the assumed strong materialism of psychology is probably more controversial here than in other areas. Nonetheless, the careful studies, testing and measuring people's perceptions and understandings, can bring highly useful insights into what our minds do.

So far, our examination of psychology has not specifically examined any of its spiritual implications. The fact is that psychology has often been deliberately, and aggressively, materialistic in its approach—that is, denying the existence of anything that cannot be explained by some material or physical mechanism; and denying any explanation of the human mind that resorts to supernatural concepts like 'God' or 'soul'.

Does this mean that psychology, no matter how accurate it might be on minor details, will inevitably conflict with Christianity?

## — *Part 3* —

# PSYCHOLOGY
# AND THE MEANING
# OF LIFE

Christianity and psychology have had a tense relationship since psychology first began to gain public notice. Those who have studied psychology at university may have experienced open ridicule from psychology lecturers, or at least a denigration of Christian belief included as part of the lecture schedule. The old stereotype of the German psychologist usually includes a very 'clinical' approach to religious belief, treating it as a quaint and curious phenomenon, not anything to be taken as *true*. Indeed, some religious bodies have even taken up psychological ideas in place of religious ones, thinking the psychological ideas are more 'advanced' and therefore more likely to be correct.[1] Is this unavoidable? Will psychology always, fundamentally, be opposed to the Christian world view?

## 1

## CHRISTIAN AND PSYCHOLOGICAL
## VIEWS OF THE MIND

First of all, we need to be clear what we are talking about. If by 'psychology' we merely mean 'the study of the mind', then there is no essential conflict. Whatever the structure of the mind is, that is what it is. If it is built in a certain way, then that is how it is built, and either a Christian or

---

1    For instance, the Vatican now considers some conditions that used to be regarded as demon possession should now be understood as psychological illness.

a non-Christian who has studied it accurately will perceive it that way. A triangle still has three sides whether a Christian or a non-Christian looks at it; the mind has certain structures no matter who looks at it.

The problem is, the mind is far more complicated than a triangle, and a lot of the data is very confusing. There is still a huge amount of experimental testing to be done before psychologists can have a comprehensive model of the mind. We still know too little. Therefore, it is possible for someone to present a theory of the mind that is largely a matter of their presuppositions, and there may be no data as such to refute it. Responsible psychologists will recognize this and reject the theory as too broad for the amount of data available. However there is a big world out there, of people with varying levels of expertise, coming up with theories of the mind. Many of these theories may well reject any Christian concepts, simply because the author of the theory does so.

Our other problem is: What exactly is a 'Christian' concept of the mind? Most people would suggest that this involves issues of soul or spirit. Is there a non-material part of the mind which can never be reduced to mere mechanism? Is this part of the mind something which the mechanist psychologist will always exclude, meaning that the Christian can never accept his or her theories?

Certainly the Bible insists we have a soul, but we are not told whether this is something entirely different from our physical bodies or not. Whatever it is, it is our essential self, our seat of personality and self-identity. Is this some immaterial substance that survives after death? It could be. But we must remember that many of our ideas about the immortal soul come from Greek philosophy, not the Bible. It is an ancient Greek teaching that the immortal soul goes on after the physical body is dead. The Bible teaches that our physical bodies will be *resurrected*, and that we will have these resurrected bodies in heaven. So is our soul something separate from these physical bodies? There is no need to think that it is; but then again, there is no need to think that it isn't. The fact is that we have a soul, and we are known by God.

Coming back to psychology, does it matter if some psychological theory denies an immaterial soul? Probably not, because the kind of soul the theory denies is more likely to be the soul of Greek and later philosophy, rather than the soul spoken of in the Bible. Even if we are entirely material, God still is the Creator and Lord of all, who sustains and upholds all things by his powerful word, and who enters into relationship with us. These are matters psychology can never (rationally) deny because it is not in a position to speak about them.

There is another, more insidious way in which psychology is used to attack Christianity. That is, certain psychologists in a rather condescending way have 'explained' religion as a transferring of the father-figure to something infinite, or as part of the progression of civilization, or some such idea. This assumes that Christian statements are not true, but that so many humans have believed in them because it was a necessary part of coping with the world, or living in society, or whatever. In this way religious belief is 'explained away' without ever having to consider its claims as real truth-claims.

Of course, the fundamental flaw in these arguments is: What if they are wrong? The psychological explanation does provide one possible explanation for religious impulses, but there is another, equally valid, and many would say more plausible explanation: namely, that humans have a religious impulse because there really is a God. On what grounds can psychologists possibly argue that they are right and Christians are wrong at this point? There can be no possible laboratory experiment that will settle the matter, nor any purely theoretical argument. The 'test' would have to include an examination of the Christian truth-claims regarding the life and death and resurrection of Jesus; but this is something outside the discipline of psychology, about which psychology therefore has nothing to say.

C. S. Lewis wrote tellingly on this point in *The Pilgrim's Regress*. The classic psychological 'explanations' of Christianity are either irrational in themselves or only half-true, argued Lewis. For example, while it is perfectly reasonable to say that our love for God as Father in some way resembles our love for human fathers, who is to say which is a reflection or copy of which? Psychology *assumes* the doctrine of God's non-existence (without demonstrating it), and asserts that belief in a heavenly father is a copy or projection of our desire for a better human father. Might it not be just as rational (if not more so) to claim that the lesser was a copy of the greater? Furthermore, the equally common argument that we only believe in God because we wish him to be there (as a 'wish-fulfilment') of course cuts both ways. Is it not just as likely (if not more so) that the atheistic psychologist has assumed and asserted the non-existence of God because he *doesn't* wish him to be there?

⟞ 2 ⟝

## CHRISTIANS STUDYING PSYCHOLOGY

It is undoubtedly true that psychology, as a community of scientists and therapists, does include elements which are hostile to Christians. There are many non-Christian psychologists who feel that their psychology denies Christianity, and who will use it to argue against Christianity; or who regard Christianity as a contributing factor to their patient's neurosis from which they should be delivered. Does this mean there is a problem for Christians *studying* psychology?

There is no essential problem in the ideas themselves. As we have seen, psychology in its purest sense aims to uncover the structures of the mind, *whatever* they are. If the real structures are discovered, then they are true for the non-Christian as well as the Christian. The Christian will have the additional knowledge that these structures are made by God; knowledge which is, sadly, excluded by the non-Christian (sadly for themselves, for their quest for knowledge will never be complete). The Christian will have a fuller appreciation of the mind; but the knowledge that the two share on a purely pragmatic basis will be the same.

It is true that some theories have made specific claims which are contrary to Christianity—for instance, the Rogerian idea that humans are fundamentally good. In this case, we must say that psychology has simply got it wrong. It is not surprising that, since this view is wrong, it can be demonstrated to be wrong in empirical studies. From such studies many psychologists, both Christian and non-Christian, have concluded that Rogerian therapy has fundamental problems.

It is also true that many psychology departments are harsh on Christians, but this is a social problem, not a problem with the study of psychology itself. Researchers and lecturers are human, and suffer human biases. It may be that the psychology is taught to students in an atmosphere that is very anti-Christian, however unfair that may be. Just as there is a myth at large that science undermines Christianity, psychology students are often taught that psychology disproves 'old-fashioned' beliefs like Christianity.

However as with any science, psychology *cannot* undermine Christianity. If it remains scientific, it will study the data that is there. It cannot prove that the mind was not created by God, or that it is not upheld by God. All psychological researchers can discover is what the mind is like now. And what a tremendous feat that would be, to be able to understand the amazing workings of the human mind! Our minds are so powerful, so mysterious in what they seem to be capable of doing and learning, it would be a marvellous triumph of science to be able to understand how we do all these amazing things. If we were ever to discover that, what glory this would shine on the God who created them!

In fact, if Christians are interested in studying God's creation at all, they surely should be drawn to the one creature God decided to have a relationship with. Many Christians already understand the wonder of studying God's creation through physics, chemistry or biology, wanting to appreciate the intricacies of God's creativity. How fitting is it for Christians to study man himself!

Psychology has a reputation for being anti-Christian, because so many anti-Christians have pursued it. However this is no reason for Christians to shy away from it. Rather, surely this is all the more reason for Christians to study psychology. It is fitting for God's creatures to study God's marvellous creativity; the anti-Christians who study it, however brilliant and painstaking they may be, will never appreciate the human mind fully.

## ⊰ 3 ⊱
## INTEGRATING CHRISTIANITY
## AND PSYCHOLOGY

Do we, then, need to find an 'integration' of psychology and Christianity, as many Christian books have argued? This is a curious term. It is recognised by such authors that psychology and Christianity both provide explanations for our very selves, our motivations and actions—fundamental explanations that seem to be competing. However as in so many other sciences, this underestimates the power of God. *No* mechanistic, scientific explanation is actually fundamental. *However* our minds work, they were still created by God.

Without this understanding, there will never be a totally comprehensive, fundamental explanation of human beings. With every neurone and every thought explained, there will still be something missing—namely, what it all means. Humans are not just elegant machines, however complex. We are created beings, created for a purpose and in the image of God. Our minds work the way they do because they were made to serve the purposes of God; and they have the flaws they do because we rebel against our purpose. Any 'integration' of psychology with Christianity would have to be within this fundamental framework.

A proposed 'integration', then, that does away with basic Christian concepts such as sin or evil—replacing them with psychological concepts such as illness, or failure to reach self-realisation—is no integration at all. What the Bible tells us about human minds is not an alternative to psychology; it is the basis for true psychology. The sinfulness of human minds is something that can be empirically demonstrated (studies on such things as selfishness and lying have shown this); but sinfulness will not make sense unless seen within the context of God's revelation. The purely empirical does not tell us enough. What is it all *about*—this is information that comes from elsewhere.

## ⊷4⊷

# THE ESSENCE OF PSYCHOLOGY

What, then, shall we say is the 'essence' of psychology? Psychology is an attempt to study the mind on materialistic, or originally mechanical, principles. To a large extent, psychology began as a protest against the vitalism of many biological theories; the idea that some mysterious force was the energy behind biological outcome. The early psychologists campaigned for this to be replaced by a mechanical explanation, with no mysterious forces.

Ever since, psychology has been beset by the problem of what to do with the mysterious, with the fact, for example, that some aspects of our mental function seem incapable of being reduced to a physical or material cause. Once vitalism was banished, there was the problem of gestalt theory, for example—which, while not drawing on any mysterious or spiritual force as such, still insisted there was more in the whole than the sum of its parts. This did not fit easily into the strictly reductionist theories which considered the proper object of study for psychology to be discrete, quantifiable aspects of brain function. Behaviourism fought more specifically against concepts of mind, sticking in its most famous form to strict observation of what stimuli produced what response, and dismissing as improper speculation any consideration of what 'thinking' was going on in between. Now that cognitive psychology is quite happy to accept thinking minds, there is still the uncomfortable and so far

69

intractable problem of consciousness.

This may be no more than an interesting aspect of the history of psychology. However it is also the case that psychology has had a history of being anti-God. Not only has the rejection of various aspects of the 'mysterious' in psychology been mistaken for a rejection of God; in many cases, it is very tempting to conclude that the rejection of God is what drove many individual psychologists to the fervent rejection of the mysterious. For materialism is held with a fervour that appears to be far beyond what is necessary for a working background assumption.[2] Many prominent psychologists have been openly anti-Christian, fiercely atheistic, and use their psychological discoveries in the mistaken belief that they somehow impinge on the truth of Christianity. It is still prominent today; Nobel Prize-winner Francis Crick, for instance, begins his book *The Astonishing Hypothesis* on the explicit grounds that his work in neurophysiology does away with the religious concept of 'soul'.

This is certainly not universal. Like most scientists

---

2    For example, philosopher David Chalmers has written that there is a common objection to a dualistic consciousness, which he calls 'Don't have a clue materialism': "I don't have a clue about consciousness. It seems utterly mysterious to me. But it must be physical, as materialism must be true." Such a view, Chalmers says, is held widely although rarely in print. David J. Chalmers, *The Conscious Mind,* Oxford University Press, 1996, p.162. For more on the how all science uses materialism as a working assumption (in order to investigate 'how things work'), and yet need not go beyond this to assert that the material world is the only thing that exists, see my earlier work, *Unnatural Enemies: an introduction to science and Christianity* (Matthias Media, 1997).

with a living to make, a lot of psychologists probably do not have the time to think much beyond their next research project. Metaphysical arguments for or against a deity have virtually no impact on their work at all, and (many psychologists probably think) hardly anything to do with *them*. The materialistic reputation of psychology is, for them, a background assumption for day-to-day operation. It is the major popularisers of psychology who have created the anti-Christian aura.

In the end, psychology suffers from the assumption that man is the arbiter of all things. That is, much psychological discussion seems to have the underlying belief that if we understand *how* we think, then we'll understand *why* we think what we do. So, for instance, in the psychology of religion one tends to find the view (as mentioned above) that when we understand the role that belief in God plays in the mind and character, then we know why people believe in God. Perhaps it is comforting, giving some stability or useful for coping with uncertainty. The purpose of the belief in God, then, is to fulfil this function. However such reasoning is not valid, as a moment's thought will demonstrate—it would be akin to saying that the only reason I believe in the existence of my mother is because of the nurturing role she played in my upbringing.

It could be that people believe in God because God is really there. The reason might be external reality, not just internal functionalism. It could be that not everything psychology studies will prove to have complete explanations within the person, or within the social influences that play on the person. It could be that morality, relationships and other aspects of humanity that psychology describes cannot be fully understood without their external reality being accepted. Relationships are not just a matter of our wishful thinking about our desire to reproduce and survive. They are a reflection of the fact that the real God values relationships above all else, and made us to be in relationship with him and each other. Without that truth, the human craving and contradictory attitudes to relationships will not make complete sense.

# CHRISTIANS AND MENTAL ILLNESS

We have already seen how Christians may sometimes feel uncomfortable about psychology, especially when it is used (wrongly) as a stick to beat God with. But there is another way in which Christians can feel uncomfortable about psychology. Is it all right for Christians to seek counselling for mental problems? This can be a scary prospect for many Christians. After all, many of the commands in the Bible appear to relate to emotional or mental life. We are told that we should be joyful; that the Christian life is not burdensome; that we should love others. If these are not true in our lives, then are we not just being disobedient? Surely striving against sin is the answer, not counselling?

The problem with discussions like this is that so many very different issues become jumbled together. Let us try to untangle a few.

First of all, it is easy to read emotional language into the Bible when it is not necessarily there. Consider the command to 'love'. In our modern parlance, 'love' is generally taken to refer to a feeling of affection or even overwhelming devotion to someone. However that is not necessarily what the Bible is talking about. In fact, most of the 'love' language in the Bible is talking about *action*, not feeling at all. God loved us in that he sent his Son to die for us. This is not saying that God feels emotionally affectionate towards us. It is not saying that he does not, either; it is not commenting on God's emotional state at all. It is a simple statement of fact, that God sent his son to die for us; that selfless action is what is meant by 'love'.

So when we are commanded to love others, we do not *have* to have a certain feeling towards them. You can love someone whom you actively dislike; by serving them, and putting their needs ahead of yours. (The feeling of dislike is not a good one, and hopefully and with prayer it will diminish; but it does not stop you from loving someone.)

But what of the command to have joy? Here it seems we have an essentially emotional word. And what of the statement that the Christian life is not burdensome? What if you feel that it is?

If we truly understood and believed the truth of the gospel, we would be joyful and we would not find any of God's commands burdensome. However there are various things that stop us from fully believing God's truth. The first and most obvious barrier is sin. In our wilful disobedience, we exchange God's truth for a lie and refuse to accept his commands.

The only way to lift this barrier is through the power of the Holy Spirit. It is only then that the veil can be lifted and our hearts and minds can comprehend the gift of the gospel. Then the spirit will continue to work in us as our minds are transformed to be more like Christ's.

However while sin is the fundamental barrier between us and our joy in God, other things can prevent us from fully taking up God's commands. This is a practical matter in a fallen world; things do not work perfectly here. One of the symptoms of being in a fallen world is that sickness is prevalent. So for instance, we are to care for each other; but a person who is chronically ill and bedridden will, practically speaking, be able to do far less for other people than the person who is well. Illness of any sort makes us less able to live as God wants us too. This is a purely practical matter, not an issue of godliness at all. The bedridden person will seek medical treatment, and if he or she is cured we can rejoice; this person will now be able to live a fuller and happier life, the sort of life God intended for us all.

Just as physical illness can rob us of some of our capacity to live well, so can mental illness. Again, this is not a matter of godliness; it is a direct parallel of some physical disability simply preventing us from doing something. If a person has a severe anxiety disorder, that person may be simply unable to relate to other Christians. If a person is suffering from depression, he or she will not be able to feel joyful and everything will seem a burden. These people may well be able to grasp the truths of the gospel intellectually; but the barrier of the mental illness stops the full enjoyment and living out of those truths.

Christianity is not a mental cure. It can relieve us of serious worries, about life after death, about our destiny, about the pain and seeming hopelessness of the world. It tells us, certainly, what the answers are to these things. However if our minds are not working properly—if our knowledge is not filtering through correctly to the rest of our beliefs—then our minds need treatment, regardless of how much truth we 'know'.

Seeking therapy is not self-centred and self-indulgent,

any more than going to hospital for a broken leg is. Like anything, it can become self-indulgent if you overdo it. But we don't accuse people of self-indulgence when they seek treatment for a broken leg. Mental illness can be far more debilitating and destructive of life and Christian relationships, but somehow going to a doctor about it is somehow seen by some as shameful!

If you suspect you might benefit from help, ask your doctor. For whatever reason, depression and other mental illnesses appear to be increasing in frequency in our society; don't think that you're simply giving in to modern self-absorption by seeking treatment for it. On the contrary, good treatment for depression stops self-absorption and allows you to think of and relate to others again.

It has been suggested that if Christian churches were acting in a more loving way, then a lot of professional counselling would be unnecessary. There may be something in that. It may be that Christians are not caring enough for each other, spending time with each other and sharing their burdens. Some problems may be helped by having a sympathetic ear, a shoulder to cry on, or help in other ways (taking care of the screaming kids, lending a holiday house). Certainly church members should do all they can to look after one another. However even in the most supportive church, there may still be mental problems that require specific cures, and which the church may not be able to supply. Sometimes a sympathetic ear is not enough. Sometimes professional treatment is necessary.

What kind of treatment is it all right for Christians to seek?

Psychotherapy is problematic, as has already been shown. Its claims are largely untestable, and it may or may not help. There is nothing wrong in trying this kind of therapy if it appeals to you, but some caution is called for.

Cognitive-behavioural therapy has a stronger reputation. It has techniques to change your thoughts and behaviour from wrong (unhelpful) to right (helpful) ones. As we have already discussed, what actually constitutes *right* thoughts is very subjective, and dependent upon what the therapist considers to be right thoughts. However, Christians have a great advantage here, because the Bible gives essential information. It tells us what is good and right, and what things are good to dwell upon. We know from the Bible that good thoughts revolve around concepts like respecting and caring for others, trying to resolve conflict peacefully, not keeping a grudge, forgiving, valuing oneself as a person created and redeemed by God rather than because of achievements. By and large, these are the things that cognitive-behavioural therapy recommends, although without the theological context. It is not surprising that this should be so, because the people who live by them *do* demonstrate the best lives, in general—that is, the most content with circumstances, unburdened by excessive anxiety and fear, and so on.

In fact, the Bible can inform cognitive-behavioural therapy to make it even more helpful. Take for instance the fear, 'When I get up to give the talk I'm going to make a total fool of myself'. A standard therapeutic challenge might be: 'No-one's ever told me I looked foolish in the past; and even if I do make a fool of myself this time, so what? One incident does not define my entire life.' Such challenges substitute rational responses for the initial, irrational one.

However the Christian has a yet more powerful challenge: 'God still values me and has a place for me in heaven regardless of whether I make a fool of myself today'. That is, believing the Bible is one of the best aids for mental health you can find. Think about it—if you *really* believed—absorbed, accepted, made your habitual thought—what the Bible tells you, you would be a long way towards mental health in just about anyone's definition. Dwell for a moment on the fact that God himself loved you enough to die for you, and that eternity in heaven is awaiting us. Can you understand now how Paul can describe himself as content whatever the circumstances?[1]

Most people, however, have to some degree absorbed wrong beliefs from the world, which conflict with what the Bible says. Until the wrong beliefs are identified and actively challenged, they will stay there. So reading the Bible—actually studying and understanding its content, and taking it seriously as the truth about reality—is good

---

1    Notice that Paul still felt negative emotions, and had many ups and downs. Being mentally healthy is not the same as being happy all the time. However it is a matter of being able to accept what life holds without falling to pieces, without sinking into overwhelming depression, and being able to continue functioning.

mental therapy. If you had as your bed-rock assumptions about life that God is in control of all things; that he loves you and values you enough to die for you; that money, power, looks or achievement will not bring satisfaction; that the best thing you can do is devote your life to God and live by his commandments; that God is to be feared, not men; then you will have achieved most of what therapy tries to achieve for you. If you behave in a way commanded by the Bible; if you don't let the sun go down on your anger, if you are slow to anger and quick to forgiveness, if you listen, if you are honest, if you love your enemies and leave revenge to God—these behaviours are all the kinds of things that therapy tries to get you to do. This is the way to a calm and realistic life.

It may be, however, that your false belief is so deeply entrenched and unrecognized that the regular routine of teaching and Bible reading does not shake it, no matter how good the teaching is. It may be that this false belief has so shaken your confidence and upset your thought patterns that you simply can't identify it and get rid of it on your own. If so, you may be helped by therapy which teaches you specific techniques to find and challenge these wrong beliefs. There is nothing mystical or mysterious about these techniques; they are simply learning strategies, like strategies for memorizing study notes or studying more effectively. Going to a specialist psychologist in order to learn these things may be simply a practical decision, and it can help your godliness enormously if it turns out that this kind of block to your learning is at the basis of various problems.

There is a lot more that could be said about psychology and Christianity, and many good books go into the subject with considerable detail. The important thing is for Christians not to be afraid of psychology. This little introduction has covered some of the basic framework of psychological research and practice, in an effort to demystify the whole area. The key is to be discerning. We have the truth about reality in the Bible; informed with that, we can make sense of any amount of data that psychology uncovers, and appreciate the therapeutical benefits it can offer.

# ⚮ *Appendix 2* ⚮

# CHRISTIANS AND DEPRESSION

## PHILIP MITCHELL SPEAKS WITH
## GREG CLARKE ABOUT DEPRESSION

For 12 years, Professor Philip Mitchell has specialized in treating people for depression. As a psychiatrist and a Christian, he has considered mental illness and the spiritual life, and how the two might be connected. Or might not be connected, as he revealed in an interview which helps us to come to terms with the nature of this common illness.

*Professor Mitchell, what is the difference between being depressed and just feeling bad about yourself?*
Sometimes it's easy to tell the difference; sometimes you're not certain. I look for clinical indicators of depressive illness: whether the person's life is becoming impaired by these bad feelings, when it's starting to interfere with people's sleep, appetite and weight, when it's interfering with their work and concentration, they're having suicidal thoughts, they can't buck up. Those symptoms help me to sort out whether it's just life problems or whether it's more.

*So depression is an illness?*
Yes. Even though there are both psychological and physical parts to it, it makes sense to think of severe depression as an illness. There are good medical and psychological treatments that can help people get out of it.

*What proportion of the population is depressed?*
Figures vary, but over a lifetime about 15% of the popu-

85

lation are prone to getting depression on at least one occasion. So it's relatively common. Some people only have one episode, but for at least half of those who suffer depression once, it is a recurring experience.

*Is depression the sort of thing that certain personality types are likely to suffer?*

I think that's true. Anybody is vulnerable to becoming depressed, if things get difficult for them, but some personality types are more prone than others. For instance, if you tend to look for your own failings and weaknesses, if you expect disasters, you are prone to becoming depressed. People who have fragile self-esteems are prone; people who are excessively perfectionistic can be thrown when things don't go quite right; people who have long-term high levels of anxiety.

*Can you describe what it is like to be depressed?*

Patients find it quite hard to describe. They often use analogies, like there is a 'black cloud' or a 'weight' on them. They say that they just can't enjoy things any more, that they can't get the drive to do anything; they stay in bed because they just have no energy or enthusiasm. They tend to ruminate and think about their failings, their hopeless situation. But many people find it hard to communicate the experience; even very articulate people have told me how difficult it is to communicate the experience to other people.

*On the other side of the fence, what is it like to be close to someone who is depressed?*

I think it's very wearing. It never ceases to amaze me how couples stay together, particularly when it's prolonged. Even with the best of good will and human kindness, long-term depression can be a very tiring experience for a spouse or close friend. You may get little response from a depressed person, little enthusiasm, withdrawal. They don't want to interact socially and sometimes they can be quite irritable. Within a marriage, tension may be increased because the depressed person has no interest in sexual activity. So these things exacerbate the problem.

*I sometimes hear it said that depressed people ought to just 'snap out of it'. Can they do that?*

Not when the depression is severe in the way we have been talking about. If someone can snap out of it, usually they have by that stage. In general, a depressed person doesn't like the experience and if it was a matter of just getting on and doing something, they would have tried it. Sometimes people need to learn psychological ways of getting out of the depressed state. But sometimes there is a biochemical process going on that means the person isn't physically able to snap out of it, without professional help.

Often there is a mixture of the physical and the psychological. It's very rarely one or the other. The more I see depression, the more I see a complex interplay between personality, the biology of our brains and our life experience.

*So depressed people can't snap out of it, but they also can't explain very easily what is actually troubling them. It's a very frustrating illness!*

Absolutely. It's hard for people who haven't dealt with it professionally to have any idea what it's like to be depressed. So people have this difficulty understanding it, and this tendency to think that the person should be able to get out of it, and the depressed person has difficulty explaining the experience and feels frustrated and stigmatized when people are telling them to snap out of it, because they know they can't snap out of it. There is enormous tension.

*I suppose the big question is, for both the depressed person and those around them, can depression be cured?*

Most people with depression can either be cured or significantly helped by available treatments. These days, we have very good treatments. We can't help everybody, but we can help the vast majority of people we see.

*Is it always a long term cure, or can it happen quickly?*

It varies. Often within a few weeks many people have benefited significantly. Some forms of depression require more long-term psychological treatment, others respond very quickly to medication. And there are grades in between.

*Is depression like alcoholism, where you can get it under control but never really be beyond its reach?*

For most people, that's probably a realistic comparison.

I tell people that they are always going to be prone to becoming depressed, so they need to be wary about relapses in the future. They need to be sensible about their medications, learn techniques to help them, think about whether there are aspects of their lives that they need to change. We can't always prevent future episodes, but we can usually make them less likely.

The poet Les Murray recently has been very public about coming out of his depression. It's interesting that some of the best poetry is written by people who have been depressed. Look at William Cowper—a Christian poet and hymn writer who wrote some of his most moving material during periods of profound depression. So depression can be both creative and destructive.

*This raises an important issue for Christians. How do we connect our mental and our spiritual lives?*

Cowper became very doubting at times, during his depression. One thing many Christian patients say is that God seems very distant during such periods. I've come to accept that as part of the depressive experience rather than a problem with their faith. I've seen people with a very deep faith, who yearn to be close to God, and who when depressed feel very barren and remote from God. For instance, J. B. Phillips, the Bible translator, was profoundly depressed for much of his adult life. He has described this sense of distance from God.

That is very distressing for Christians. They begin to worry that it is a lack of faith or lack of spiritual growth.

But having seen it enough, I think it is just an expression of the depressive experience. Many Christians also feel that depression is a sign of weakness, of spiritual inadequacy, and they have a strong sense of guilt. Unfortunately, I think that often the church, explicitly or implicitly, has encouraged that—that if you have depression it's a reflection on your spiritual life. This adds an incredible burden to people who are already feeling guilty and self-critical. It's a bit like Job's encouragers, who basically made him feel worse.

*Why does there seem to be a large number of depressed people in our churches?*
It's often the more sensitive people who become depressed, and there are often a lot of obsessional and sensitive people in churches. My experience is that there is a lot of depression in our congregations and that we don't handle it at all well. We often infer, explicitly or implicitly, that the Christian shouldn't have the experience of depression—that it's not part of the victorious Christian life. And that causes enormous guilt and makes people less likely to talk about it. I think we have a lot of silent suffering going on in our churches. People just aren't getting helped, because they feel guilty about having depression. We need to bring out into the open the fact that depression is a common experience, even within the church. And that being a Christian doesn't stop you from getting depression. And that having depression is no more a failing than having diabetes.

In general, the church deals very badly with mental illness. In the middle ages, it was considered demon possession; in the late 20th century it's considered a symptom of spiritual inadequacy. But it isn't necessarily either of these things.

*Are people in very demanding ministries especially prone?*
They are prone; I don't know about especially. They are in line for so many of the factors that contribute to depression: burn-out, demoralisation, excessive demands, not looking after your own emotional needs, not having time to yourself. I see some of the casualties, and often by then it's too late because someone has resigned from the ministry or become completely disillusioned. And it's all too hidden, too hush-hush. We're dealing with it no better than the secular world; in some ways we're doing worse.

*What then are the ways that a depressed person can be helped, both by individuals and by the church?*
Well, especially in the early days, one can be supportive, help people get back into their lives—those normal things of friendship and support, being a sounding board, willing to listen to difficulties. These things might be sufficient to alleviate the early experience of depression.

But if we're looking at a fully-formed depression that's been going on for a while, the person should be encouraged to seek proper professional help. That doesn't always mean a psychiatrist; it might mean a GP or a counsellor. Just someone with the skills and training to help. So that's the first thing, when the support networks have been stretched to the limit.

While that process is happening, it's important to be around for the depressed person, accepting the fact that it might be a frustrating experience until that person picks up. Not feeling that you have to do everything yourself. There has to be a point where a friend accepts that they can't provide everything the person needs. That point is usually indicated by signs like someone crying constantly, their work falling apart, withdrawing inexplicably, perhaps losing weight. These things indicate that the depression is getting severe.

*Finally, do you think depression has become more of a problem today than it used to be?*
It's an area of debate. There's no doubt that depression has always existed. The old Greek medical writers are clearly describing patients with depression. There was a book written in the 17th century called *The Anatomy of Melancholy* which described what we would call depressed patients. So it goes back through the ages; it's part of the general human experience.

The issue is whether it has become more frequent. People have looked at the occurrence of depression in groups of people born in different decades in this century, and the frequency of occurrence seems to go up as the decades continue. People born in the 60s are more prone to depression than those at similar ages, but born in the 30s. Now, the significance of that is debated. It could be that people in recent decades simply have become more willing to admit to their depression, hence the higher rate of reports. Or it could be true that it is becoming a more common experience, and presumably that reflects changes in society. What those changes are is a very difficult question to answer.

*So it's hard to say whether the loneliness of urban living is a major factor?*
Well yes, and it's a very interesting area of debate. The World Health Organization has released predictions of the impact of different illnesses over the next century. They are saying that depression will be the 21st century's most disabling condition, in terms of the impact on the individual, frequency and cost to society, on a worldwide basis. That survey included all medical conditions, including cancer and heart disease. So there is a recognition that it is a very prevalent condition, and that it is a very disabling condition to have. Whatever is causing it, we're going to have to deal with it.

(Reprinted from *The Briefing*, Issue 198, a publication of Matthias Media).

*Other Matthias Media resources from the same author...*

# The essence of the Reformation

Corruption in the church. Political turmoil and intrigue. A clash of new ideas and ancient pagan religions. Courageous and extraordinary individuals. Doctrinal disputes that were matters of life and death.

These things and more make up what is often called the 'Reformation', that tumultuous period of European history ranging from around 1517 to the turn of the century. Unfortunately, the events, people and ideas are generally not well known today, even though in many ways, the Reformation made our modern world what it is. It provided the thinking and beliefs that shaped intellectual and religious endeavour for centuries to come, down to the present day.

In this short book, Kirsten Birkett brings us the essence of the Reformation—the social and religious soil in which it grew, the events and people which shaped it, the ideas and doctrines for which many of them died.

ORDERING DETAILS:

*Australia*

Matthias Media
Telephone: +61-2-9663 1478
Facsimile: +61 2-9662 4289
Email:
<sales@matthiasmedia.com.au>

*United Kingdom*

St Matthias Press
Telephone: +44-181-942-0880
Facsimile: +44-181-942-0990
Email:
<MattMedia@compuserve.com>

www.matthiasmedia.com.au

# An introduction to science and Christianity

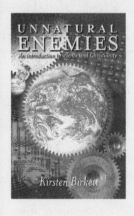

UNNATURAL ENEMIES

"History records that whenever science and orthodoxy have been fairly opposed, the latter has been forced to retire from the lists, bleeding and crushed, if not annihilated; scotched if not slain." So argued Thomas Huxley, one of the nineteenth century's great champions of science against Christian belief.

Was he right? Are science and Christianity destined to be bitter enemies? Is it possible to be a Christian and a good scientist?

In this compellingly readable introduction to the subject, Kirsten Birkett looks at both science and Christianity, clearly explaining what both are about, and dispelling many common confusions and misunderstandings. She argues that while there are no necessary grounds for the two to be at war, there is still reason to think that the conflict might continue.

For all devotees of science—Christian or non-Christian, professional, student or lay—Dr Birkett's perspective as both a Christian and an historian of science sheds new light on these perennial questions.